Nine Ducks Nine

Written and illustrated by

Sarah Hayes

WALKER BOOKS
LONDON

This book is dedicated to the memory of Ben,
a boy who loved animals

First published 1990 by
Walker Books Ltd, 87 Vauxhall Walk
London SE11 5HJ

© 1990 Sarah Hayes

First printed 1990
Printed by South China Printing Co. (1988) Ltd., Hong Kong

British Library Cataloguing in Publication Data
Hayes, Sarah
Nine ducks nine.
I. Title
823'.914 [J]

ISBN 0-7445-1501-7

Nine ducks nine walked out in line.

Mr Fox was watching.

One duck ran away,
down to the rickety bridge.

Eight ducks eight sat on the gate.

Mr Fox came through the woods.

One duck ran away,

down to the rickety bridge.

Seven ducks seven took off together.

Mr Fox came out of the woods.

One duck flew away,

down to the rickety bridge.

Six ducks six did balancing tricks.

Mr Fox came closer.

One duck ran away,

down to the rickety bridge.

Five ducks five began to dive.
Mr Fox came closer.
One duck swam away,
down to the rickety bridge.

Four ducks four reached the shore.

Mr Fox came closer and closer.

One duck flew away,

down to the rickety bridge.

Three ducks three flew into a tree.

Mr Fox came closer and closer.

One duck flew away,

down to the rickety bridge.

Two ducks two had things to do.

Mr Fox came even closer.

One duck crept away,

to the end of the rickety bridge.

One duck one sat in the sun,
all alone on the rickety bridge.

Mr Fox came right up close and…

Mr Fox pounced!

The rickety bridge broke and
SPLASH!
Mr Fox fell into the river.

Nine ducks nine swam back in line.
Mr Fox went home to his den
and never chased those ducks again.